WORLD WAR 3:
Our Future?
2022-2023

The truth about the war in Ukraine, the influence on our economy & global markets

Economic Crisis – Hyperinflation – Food Shortage

Truth Leaks Books

Disclaimer

How did it start?

These conflicts go way back. The ancestors of Ukrainians, Russians and Belarusians lived together from the 9th to the 13th centuries in the Kiev Rus, a grand principality. A Mongol invasion ended that unity. Ukraine then passed in pieces through the hands of numerous powers, including the Polish-Lithuanian Commonwealth, the Ottoman Empire, Austria-Hungary and the Russian Empire.

The first time Ukrainians declared independence was in 1918, shortly after the Russian Revolution. That independence did not last long and Ukraine was absorbed into the Soviet Union, as the Ukrainian Soviet Socialist Republic. This was given almost the same borders as today's Ukraine after World War II. Soviet leader Khrushchev transferred the Crimean peninsula from the Russian Soviet Republic to the Ukrainian Soviet Republic in 1954.

Ukraine suffered greatly during the period of the Soviet Union. When Ukrainian peasants resisted the collectivization of farmland, Josef Stalin punished Ukraine by deliberately provoking a famine. Millions of Ukrainians perished.

Ukraine has been independent since 1991. In that year, 90 percent of the population voted to secede from the Soviet Union.

What about the language?

There is one official language in Ukraine: Ukrainian. The language is related to Russian, but differs significantly. Compare it to the difference between German and English.

Because of the history in the Russian Empire and the Soviet Union, most Ukrainians also speak Russian. Moscow tried to Russify the Ukrainians by suppressing Ukrainian and imposing Russian. Thus, it was dangerous for Ukrainian writers to publish in their own language.

The current government is promoting Ukrainian with a 2019 language law. This makes Ukrainian the mandatory language in schools and forces TV and radio stations to broadcast mainly in Ukrainian.

Over three-quarters of the population lists Ukrainian as their first language in polls. For 20 percent, Russian is the first language. Russian still prevails in eastern and southern Ukraine.

Why is Ukraine so important to President Putin?

Putin has often described the collapse of the Soviet Union as "the greatest tragedy of the twentieth century." It was also probably the greatest tragedy in his own life.

It ended his career as a KGB spy in East Germany, where, according to the new book Putin's People, written by investigative journalist Catherine Belton, he was likely involved in assassination attempts by the Stasi, the secret East German police. While the West celebrated victory in the Cold War, Putin, by his own account, had to make ends meet as a cab driver.

As far as Putin is concerned, former Soviet republics are still subordinate to Moscow. He believes that the countries belong to the Russian sphere of influence, whether they want it or not.

This applies most strongly to Slavic neighbors Belarus and Ukraine. Putin points to the shared history in the Kiev Rus to deny the existence of the Ukrainian nation. He said publicly for the first time in 2013 that Russians and Ukrainians are "one and the same people." Upon the annexation of Crimea, in 2014, he described Kiev as "the mother of Russian cities." "The old Rus is our common source and we cannot live without each other," Putin said.

For the Russian president, it is unacceptable for Ukraine or Belarus to turn away from Russia and choose democracy. In 2020, Putin upheld Belarusian dictator Aleksandr Lukashenko during months of peaceful demonstrations against blatant election fraud. Since then, Putin has been drawing Belarus ever closer to Russia.

After intervening against protesters in Kazakhstan in 2022 as well, Putin said he would always protect the region around Russia from "color revolutions," referring to democratic upheavals.

Why is the conflict escalating now?

In the spring of 2021, according to Western intelligence agencies, Russia gathered about 100 thousand soldiers on the border with Ukraine. Russia spoke of exercises and said it was withdrawing some of the soldiers.

But in the fall, U.S. intelligence agencies warned that Russia had not withdrawn a large portion of the soldiers and was in the process of a new troop buildup.

Russia denied attack plans, but did come up with a whole package of security demands. On December 17, 2021, Russia issued an ultimatum to the U.S. and NATO. President Putin threatened "military-technical measures" if NATO did not withdraw from Poland and the Baltic countries. He also demanded a written commitment from the U.S. and NATO that former Soviet republics, such as Ukraine, should never become members of the Western alliance. The U.S. and NATO rejected those demands, but were willing to negotiate on nuclear arms control and restrictions on military exercises.

U.S. President Biden said in January 2022 he thought Putin would invade Ukraine. On February 21, Putin announced that he would recognize the two separatist regions in eastern Ukraine, Donetsk and Luhansk, as being independent. In the speech, Putin left no doubt: it would not stop there, Ukraine belongs to Russia. Three days later, on February 24, a military attack on targets across the country followed.

What do the Ukrainian people want?

A growing majority of the 45 million Ukrainians favor joining Western alliances. Research by the sociological institute Kiis shows that 59 percent of the population wants to join NATO, 28 percent are against. Support for joining the EU is even higher.

Pro-Western attitudes are on the rise in Ukraine. At the beginning of the conflict with Russia, in 2014, a minority was still in favor of joining NATO.

There are regional differences: in the Ukrainian-speaking west there is more support for joining Western alliances than in the Russian-speaking east. But polls show that in eastern provinces support for a Western course is also growing.

What is true of Putin's claim that Western countries promised that NATO would not expand eastward? Since the Soviet Union, NATO has expanded into Eastern Europe and the Baltic countries. Seven of the eight former members of the Warsaw Pact are now NATO members.

According to Putin, the West has thus broken a promise. In late 2021, at his annual press conference, Putin said, ''No inch to the east,'' they said to us in the 1990s. And what? They cheated, they just cheated us brutally.'

Whole books have been written about the inch (2.54 centimeters), such as Not One Inch by historian Mary Elise Sarotte. These show that after the fall of the Berlin Wall, there were indeed discussions between Western leaders and Soviet leaders about a ban on NATO expansion. James Baker, then U.S. Secretary of State, asked Gorbachev in 1990 if the Soviet leader wanted assurances that NATO would "not advance an inch eastward. Gorbachev later said that Baker's suggestion paved the way for a compromise on German unification.

But no written agreement was ever reached on it. This was largely because Baker's boss, U.S. President Bush, was vehemently opposed to such an agreement. The final treaty on German unification, also signed by the Soviet Union, allowed Germany to join NATO and placed no limits on further NATO expansion.

Did Russia promise in writing never to attack Ukraine? Yes. Ukraine was a military superpower after independence with Soviet nuclear weapons. Ukraine gave up those nuclear weapons with the signing of the Budapest Memorandum in 1994, in which Ukraine received security guarantees from Russia, the United States and the United Kingdom in return.

The most important guarantee, which twenty years later would be violated by Russia: "abstention from the threat or use of force against the territorial integrity or political independence of Ukraine.

Also in 1997, through a treaty of friendship with Ukraine, Russia promised not to violate the neighboring country's borders.

How strong is the Ukrainian military?

Stronger than in 2014, when the Ukrainian army was overrun by the Russian army. Crimea was lost without firing a shot. In eastern Ukraine, Ukrainian soldiers fought in sneakers and without bulletproof vests.

But Ukraine is hopeless in a showdown with nuclear power Russia. Russia has four times more soldiers than Ukraine. The difference is even greater in the air and at sea. While Russia has 1,160 combat aircraft, Ukraine has to make do with 125.

Zelensky addresses Russian mercenaries: 'A long life is better than money'

In a recent speech, Volodimir Zelensky warned the Russian armed forces. "We are different now than we were in 2014," the Ukrainian president said in a

Facebook video about the annexation of Crimea that went 'without a fight' at the time.

Today's Ukraine, according to Zelensky, is "capable of defending itself against a large-scale invasion for 22 days.

The Ukrainian president, like a day earlier, again addressed Russian fighters. This time he warned in particular mercenaries from other countries whom he wants to save from 'the worst decision of their lives'. Zelensky said that "a long life is better than the money offered for a short one.

Ukrainian defense minister: 'You should have stopped this monster earlier'

In Ukraine, more Russian soldiers have already died in three weeks than in two Chechen wars combined, the number of deaths approaching that of ten years of war in Afghanistan.

So says Ukrainian Defense Minister Oleksii Reznikov, who this morning in the European Parliament bitterly reproached the West: "You could and should have stopped this monster earlier."

Reznikov already made a deep impression on Wednesday, according to Minister Ollongren and others, in a private video conversation with the 30 NATO defense ministers, this morning he made his story again in the European Parliament and this time publicly. ,,Eight years ago we chose Europe, and today we continue that choice armed. We see no other option but to choose civilization, democracy and basic human rights, but we are paying a terribly high price.

What the Kremlin is doing today is indescribable, Putin is the Hitler of our time. I cannot talk without emotion about the state terror we witness every day."

After which Reznikov told how entire towns and villages are being destroyed, looted and wiped off the map. ,,In Marioepol, according to local authorities, more than 20,000 people have been killed. A theater was bombed where women and children were hiding, while the monster in that plane knew what he was doing.

Aid convoys are constantly blocked and shot at. Entire families, as well as mayors who refuse to collaborate are kidnapped and murdered, an American journalist who was filming an evacuation - not an act of war, but an evacuation - was shot through the head. Russia's goal is to destroy Ukraine. You could have prevented this if you had stopped Putin earlier. Not trying to bring him to his senses but stopping him, as we are trying to do now at terrible cost."

What price has to be paid?

Reznikov then came up with some "statistics": The Ukrainian army, aided by masses of patriotic citizens, has already killed more than 14,000 Russian soldiers, disabled 450 tanks and armored cars, and shot 750 planes out of the sky. ,,We are going to continue this and we are going to win. The purpose of terror is to create fear, but we are not afraid. But at what cost? The whole world is now paying for the West's inaction."

At the conclusion of his speech, Reznikov asked the House for more military aid: anti-tank and small arms, but also air defense and weapons to shoot more planes and helicopters out of the sky.

And Western sanctions policy must be tightened much further. With anger in his voice: ,,Still companies from Switzerland, Germany and France do business with Russia. They are making money at the expense of the blood of our women and children. We are going to hand you a list of those companies."

Table of Contents

Disclaimer 1

How did it start? 2

Table of Contents................................. 12

The Russian-Ukrainian war 13

The history of war in East-Ukraine 20

A letter from Putin................................ 33

Negotiations with Russia 38

Sanctions! 41

How will the war develop? 51

8 possible outcomes 64

Putin is destroying Ukraine.................... 74

Why is Kyiv so important? 85

Swiss banks and Russian money.............. 89

Ukraine and NATO 92

Upcoming food shortages....................... 98

The Russo-Ukrainian War is an ongoing war primarily involving Russia and pro-Russian separatist forces on one side, and Ukraine and its international supporters on the other.

The first eight years of the conflict include Russia's annexation of the Crimea peninsula (2014) and the war in eastern Ukraine (2014-present) between Ukraine and Russian-backed separatists, as well as naval incidents, cyber warfare, and political tensions. The Russo-Ukrainian War began after Ukrainian President Viktor Yanukovych was deposed in February 2014 following pro-Western demonstrations and Russia subsequently occupied Crimea. This led to protests in the eastern and southern parts of Ukraine.

In the eastern Ukrainian oblasts of Donetsk and Luhansk, the protests escalated into armed conflict after rebels occupied several government buildings starting April 6, 2014, and the Ukrainian government deployed the army in response. The insurgents managed to take control of the cities of Donetsk and Luhansk, as well as the area southeast of them up to the Russian border, where they declared the self-proclaimed People's Republic of Donetsk and People's Republic of Luhansk, to become part of Russia just like Crimea.

The remaining areas in the Donbas remained under the control of the Ukrainian army.

In late 2021 and early 2022, there was a renewed upsurge in tensions. On February 22, 2022, Russian President Vladimir Putin declared that Russia recognized the self-proclaimed People's Republics of Donetsk and Luhansk, including their claims to the entire territory of Donetsk Oblast and Luhansk Oblast, respectively. A Russian invasion of all of Ukraine followed on February 24, significantly escalating the conflict.

The conflict led to a further deterioration in relations between Russia and the West, which had already been severely strained as a result of Russia's annexation of Crimea. The West accuses Russia of supporting the insurgents both financially and militarily, while the West is actually seen by Russia as responsible for the conflict getting out of hand.

The history since 1991

Even after Ukraine became an independent country upon the collapse of the Soviet Union in 1991, Russia continued to consider it part of its sphere of interest. Romanian analyst Iulian Chifu believes that with regard to Ukraine, Russia is pursuing a modernized version of the Brezhnev doctrine on "limited sovereignty," which dictates that Ukraine's sovereignty should be no greater than it was at the time of the Warsaw Pact prior to the collapse of the Soviet sphere of influence.

He bases his argument on statements by Russian leaders, who believe that Ukraine's possible integration into NATO would endanger Russia's national security.

After the collapse of the Soviet Union in late 1991, the two countries retained very close ties. At the same time, there were several sticking points, most notably Ukraine's substantial nuclear arsenal, which Ukraine had been willing to cede only after security guarantees by the nuclear powers in the Budapest Memorandum (1994).

In it, Russia (and the other signatories) gave assurances, among others, that they would respect Ukraine's territorial integrity and political independence and would not use threats or force against it. In 1999, Russia was a signatory to the Charter for European Security, where it "affirmed the inherent right of each participating state to be free to choose or modify its security arrangements, including alliance treaties, as they evolve"; both would prove worthless in 2014.

A second point of contention was the splitting of the Black Sea Fleet. Ukraine agreed to lease the port of Sevastopol so that the Russian Black Sea Fleet could continue to use it with Ukraine. From 1993, through the 1990s and 2000s, Ukraine and Russia had several gas disputes.

15

Annexation of Crimea by Russia

A few days after President Yanukovych fled the capital of Kiev in the last week of February 2014, armed men opposed to the Euromaidan movement began to take control of the Crimean peninsula. In the capital of Crimea's autonomous republic, Simferopol, and the independently governed port city of Sebastopol, home to a Russian Naval base under the 2010 Kharkiv pact, checkpoints were set up by unmarked Russian soldiers wearing green uniforms and military-grade equipment.

For Russia, Crimea was of great strategic importance because there, at Sebastopol, was a major base of the Black Sea Fleet.

Secession of Crimea threatened. However, most Crimean Tatars (about 12.1% of the Crimean population) opposed Russian intervention and supported the new rulers in Kiev. The Mejlis of the Crimean Tatars, through Chairman Refat Chubarov, called for the formation of self-defense squads.

Russian intervention

In Crimea, dozens of armed men occupied the parliament building in the regional capital Simferopol on February 27, 2014. They raised the Russian flag. Two airports near Simferopol and Sebastopol were occupied by Russian soldiers.

The Ukrainian state television building in Simferopol was also occupied by a pro-Russian militia or Russian military. The actions were intended to "preserve the position on the Black Sea." The United Nations Security Council met in New York in response to these events.

On March 1, President Putin received authorization from the Russian Federation Council to deploy military forces in Ukraine. Putin himself had requested this. According to him, the troops were needed in Crimea to protect ethnic Russians and the Black Sea Fleet. The Kremlin spoke of deploying military forces on the territory of Ukraine. That left open the possibility of deploying troops elsewhere than Crimea. Three hours later, Acting President Oleksandr Turchynov announced that the Ukrainian military had mobilized. He warned Russia that any military action in Ukraine would lead to war.

On March 6, 2014, the Crimean parliament agreed to a decree that Crimea became part of Russia. In preparation for this, independence was declared on March 11.

A referendum on joining Russia was held on March 16, 2014, with the vast majority of the population voting in favor of joining. However, Ukraine, the European Union, and the United States did not recognize this referendum, considering that prior negotiations with

Ukraine were necessary, and that the Russian military presence would interfere with the freedom of the vote.

Annexation

On March 18, 2014, it was officially announced that Crimea had been annexed by Russia. This is recognized outside of Russia only by Belarus.On March 24, the Ukrainian government decided to evacuate all of its soldiers and their families from Crimea.

Agreements and ceasefires

On September 5, 2014, under international pressure, a first ceasefire, the Minsk Agreement, was agreed upon, but was poorly observed by both sides. A new ceasefire agreement, Minsk II, was reached on February 12, 2015. This agreement was reasonably respected for a time, but violence flared up again more strongly during 2016.

Aftermath

On January 25, 2016, the Ukrainian government announced that Ukraine would be suing Russia over the annexation of Crimea. According to the Ukrainian news agency UNIAN, the Ukrainian government would bring the case before the International Tribunal for the Law of the Sea and the International Court of Justice, among others.

Since the annexation, land expropriations and other types of confiscations, not infrequently referred to as "nationalizations," have been taking place on a large scale in Crimea.

To open up Crimea, the Russian Federation opened the Kerch Bridge across the Kerch Strait. On November 25, 2018, the Russian Navy blocked this strait, which forms the passage between the Black Sea and the Sea of Azov.

The history of war in East-Ukraine

The War in Eastern Ukraine is an armed conflict in the Donets Basin (the Donbass) in eastern Ukraine between separatist groups supported by the Russian military and the Ukrainian military.

The conflict arose in the spring of 2014, after Ukrainian President Viktor Yanukovych was deposed in February following pro-Western demonstrations and Russia occupied Crimea. This then led to protests in the eastern and southern parts of Ukraine. In the eastern Ukrainian oblasts of Donetsk and Luhansk, the protests escalated into armed conflict after rebels occupied several government buildings starting April 6, 2014, and the Ukrainian government deployed the army in response.

The rebels managed to take control of the cities of Donetsk and Luhansk, as well as the area southeast of them up to the Russian border, where they declared the People's Republic of Donetsk and People's Republic of Luhansk to become part of Russia as Crimea. The remaining areas in Donbass remained under the control of the Ukrainian military.

On September 5, 2014, under international pressure, a first ceasefire was agreed upon, the Minsk Agreement. However, this agreement was poorly respected by both sides. A new ceasefire, Minsk II, was reached on February 12, 2015. This agreement was reasonably respected for a time, but violence flared up again more strongly during 2016.

The conflict further deteriorated relations between Russia and the West, which had already been severely strained as a result of the annexation of Crimea.

The West accused Russia of supporting the insurgents both financially and militarily, while the West was actually seen by Russia as responsible for the conflict getting out of hand. In the years between 2014 and 2022, the West, especially the U.S., supported Ukraine militarily with weapons, training, joint exercises, intelligence and money.

Within a broader framework, the war in eastern Ukraine is part of the Russian-Ukrainian war. The Russian-Ukrainian conflict of 2021-2022 is an escalation of the latter war. On February 21, 2022, President Putin recognized the self-proclaimed People's Republics of Donetsk and Luhansk, and three days later, Russia invaded Ukraine, resulting in a direct war between the two countries.

Preface

In the 2004 Ukrainian presidential elections, the pro-Russian Viktor Yanukovych initially emerged as the winner. However, the results of the election were not accepted by much of the population, which led to the Orange Revolution. The result was eventually declared invalid after which new elections were held. These were won by the pro-European Viktor Yushchenko. However, in the 2010 elections, the pro-Russian Yanukovych was still elected president.

On November 21, 2013, Yanukovych canceled negotiations with the European Union on a trade agreement that would allow for greater integration with Europe (the Association Agreement between the European Union and Ukraine). However, among a part of the Ukrainian population there were hopes for closer cooperation with the West, and Yanukovych created enormous misunderstanding among them with this decision.

Protests against this decision followed throughout the country, which increasingly turned into anti-government protests (Euromaidan). The protests became increasingly violent and numerous people were killed in harsh confrontations between police and insurgents. On February 19, 2014, Ukraine therefore declared a state of emergency. A few days later, Yanukovych fled Kiev. The parliament deposed the president, called new elections and appointed a new parliamentary speaker.

The unrest shifted from Kiev to Crimea in the south on February 26, 2014. The majority of the population of this peninsula, which belonged to Russia until 1954, was Russian and opposed to the change of power in Kiev. On February 27, 2014, dozens of armed men occupied the parliament building in the regional capital of Crimea Simferopol. Other important buildings were also occupied and the Ukrainian government lost its grip on the area. The United Nations Security Council met because of the annexation of Crimea, but did not reach a solution. On March 16, 2014, the parliament of Crimea held a referendum in which 95% opted for annexation to Russia.

The objectivity of the referendum was questioned worldwide and the Ukrainian government declared the referendum unconstitutional. Following the referendum, Crimea declared its independence. On March 21, Crimea and the city of Sebastopol became constituent states of Russia, a fact that both Ukraine and most other countries do not recognize to this day.

Russian minorities in Ukraine

After Yanukovych's ousting, protests against the new government and its new direction grew especially in the Donetsk and Luhansk oblasts, where a relatively large number of Russian minorities live. The Ukrainian police tried to control the situation, but barely succeeded. On April 6, 2014, residents of the Donetsk and Luhansk oblasts stormed administrative buildings. Influenced by the Annexation of Crimea, the residents of the Donetsk and Luhansk demanded a similar referendum, as had occurred in Crimea.

On April 12, government buildings in the city of Slovyansk were occupied by separatists. The organization Donetskaya Respoeblika, founded in late 2005, proclaimed the Donetsk People's Republic on April 14.

Storyline of the armed conflict

On April 13, 2014, Ukrainian Interim President Oleksandr Turchynov issued an ultimatum to end the occupation of government buildings, which had now expanded to even more cities in eastern and southern Ukraine (such as Horlivka, Kramatorsk, and Mariupol). To this end, the use of the army was kept as a stick. However, his demand remained unanswered and on April 15 the Ukrainian army was officially deployed and military actions began.

That same day, the Kramatorsk airport, which had been taken by separatists, was recaptured by the Ukrainian army. In the following weeks, the Ukrainian army managed to restore authority in several cities, but the separatists retained power in Donetsk and Luhansk, among others.

On May 11, the separatists called a referendum on Donetsk's independence. Independent observations were impossible during the referendum, but according to the separatists, 89% favored secession. The next day, Donetsk declared its independence. The same scenario repeated itself in Luhansk, leading to the proclamation of the independent People's Republic of Luhansk. Igor Girkin was proclaimed leader of the rebels, and he declared that all Ukrainian military and police members had to submit or else leave the area within 48 hours, or they would be prosecuted as terrorists. According to Ukraine and the West, the referenda had been manipulated by Russia.

Around the May 25 Ukrainian presidential election, which was not held in the separatist-occupied areas, the Ukrainian military's offensives were halted. However, after Petro Poroshenko was elected as the new president, offensives resumed. The separatists in Donetsk declared themselves at war with Ukraine after the new offensives.

The fighting continued and by the end of June at least 423 people had been killed, according to the UN. Meanwhile, the new president had unilaterally announced a ceasefire on June 8, but it did not last. On June 13, Mariupol was finally captured by the Ukrainian government. On June 18, a new cease-fire was agreed upon, but after failed negotiations, Poroshenko decided not to extend the truce.

After a final solution was out of sight, the Ukrainian army began a major new offensive. On July 5, fighting ended in Slovyansk and Kramatorsk, after which the rebels retreated to Donetsk. The army advanced further and also carried out bombing raids on the rebel camps of Donetsk.

On July 17, 2014, a Malaysia Airlines Boeing with flight number MH17 crashed near the village of Hrabove in Donetsk oblast. On board were fifteen crew members and 283 passengers, 193 of whom were of Dutch nationality. There were no survivors. It was quickly concluded that the plane must have been shot down.

According to Western analysts, the damage to parts of the plane corresponded to the impact of shrapnel from an anti-aircraft missile. In the West, the main responsibility was placed on the separatist rebels and Russia, while from the Russian side it was suggested that the Ukrainian military was guilty of accidentally downing the plane.

There was also much commotion surrounding a Russian convoy that came to provide humanitarian aid. According to Moscow, Russia was not providing military aid, but there were more and more rumors that the Russians were actively supporting the rebels.

On August 25, a counteroffensive came from the separatists who tried to hold their supply lines. The Ukrainian army was driven back in several places. The new advance of the separatists and the balance of power that subsequently emerged meant that the various parties were now willing to agree to a ceasefire. On September 1, the separatists had already made consultation possible by stating that they did not want independence, but a separate status within Ukraine. On September 5, with the Minsk Agreement, a cease-fire was declared by the various parties. The ceasefire was initially observed fairly well, although violations occurred here and there, resulting in several deaths.

In January 2015, it seemed for a while that the warring parties would come closer together through good talks. However, soon there were again numerous incidents and clashes between the Ukrainian army and the separatists, so that the ceasefire was barely observed during January and both sides threatened each other with new offensives. In response to the growing tensions and conflicts, the international community called for a new ceasefire (Minsk II) to renew the previous one.

On February 7, 2015, the treaty was signed by the various parties. In the following months, violent incidents continued to occur, but they were sporadic.

In June 2015, fierce fighting briefly flared up again, particularly near the towns of Marjinka and Shirokyne, where over 20 people were killed in a short period of time. On August 17, eight civilian deaths occurred in 24 hours and two soldiers also lost their lives.

In August 2015, German Chancellor Merkel, French President Hollande and Poroshenko called for a new ceasefire.

However, in early November, the number of incidents nevertheless increased again. On November 14, it was announced that five Ukrainian soldiers had been killed in renewed fighting over the past 24 hours.[30]

On April 29, 2016, a senior UN official reported to the UN Security Council that a total of more than 9,000 people had been killed since the conflict began. Violence in eastern Ukraine was now said to be back to the level of August 2014.

July 2016, according to a Ukrainian spokesman, was the bloodiest month since the ceasefire was declared a year and a half earlier. There was daily back and forth shooting, and on the Ukrainian army side, 41 people were reportedly killed in the period from June 27 to July 25. Several people were also killed on the side of the separatists during this period.

On September 1, 2016, a new truce came into force again. The first days after this there were no deaths; on September 9, spokesman Lysenko reported the death of a Ukrainian soldier.

On February 3, 2017, six soldiers of the Ukrainian government army were killed after another battle with the rebels, who in turn lost two civilians. According to the United Nations, the death toll had now reached 10,000.

On February 18, the foreign ministers of Russia, Ukraine, Germany and France reached a new agreement in Munich on a ceasefire, which was to take effect two days later.

In late 2017, the U.S. agreed to sell lethal weapons to Ukraine.

In early July 2019, Ukrainian President Volodymyr Zelensky, newly elected in April 2019, spoke for the first time with Russian President Vladimir Putin about the war in eastern Ukraine. In addition, the two reportedly discussed releasing prisoners and continuing expert-level talks.

In 2020, the ceasefire was reasonably maintained, with a significant decrease in the number of shots observed by the OSCE. From the end of 2021, tensions in the area rose again, partly due to the stationing of increasing numbers of Russian soldiers on the Russian-Ukrainian border.

Warring parties

The bulk of the pro-Russian resistance is formed by the Russian army and the Donbass people's militias. The militias consist of the Donbass and Luhansk militias that together form the United Forces of Novorossiya, the Russian Orthodox Army, the Army of the Southeast, and the Vostok Battalion. The Donbass and Luhansk militias have an army of 20,000, while the other militias are quite small. In addition, it is claimed by Ukraine and NATO, among others, that there are several Russian troops supporting the separatists. However, Russia itself claims that there are no troops present and that they are only volunteers.

However, this is not true according to the Ukrainian website Informnapalm.

Ukrainian side

The official army makes up the bulk of the force with about 280,000 men. In addition, paramilitaries are present with local volunteers as well as foreign volunteers. Their numbers are more difficult to estimate.

The West is not a military party to the conflict, but arms deliveries were being considered by the Americans. However, many European countries, including Germany, opposed this, believing that the conflict should be resolved diplomatically rather than militarily.

International responses to the war

NATO referred to the conflict primarily in terms of Russia's role and criticized the possible presence of weapons and troops that created a humanitarian disaster.

The European Union saw in Ukraine an important new trading partner and therefore supported the country economically and humanely. Several sanctions were imposed against Russia.

Russia saw itself as an observer of the conflict and denied involvement in its derailment. Russia, in turn, correctly accused the EU and the US of escalation. It did feel it had the right to protect Russian minorities abroad.

The United States, in particular, saw Russia as inciting events and demanded that Russia stay out of the conflict.

After great diplomatic and political support, the U.S. proceeded to supply heavy weapons to the army of Ukraine. These included Javalin missiles that were moved to the front.

Effects of the war

On a humanitarian level, the war was a disaster for Donbass residents. About 1.2 million people lost their homes and many were on the run.

According to a UN estimate in March 2015, at least 6,000 people had been killed in the conflict by then.

Internationally, Russia and the EU became entangled and several boycotts and embargoes followed on both sides.[49] Tensions between the U.S. and Russia also escalated, leading to a low point in their mutual relations.

A letter from Putin

A letter, written by Putin in June 2021 on the Zeit Online news website as preface for the war in 2022

Exactly 80 years ago, on June 22, 1941, the Nazis, having conquered all of Europe , invaded the USSR. For the Soviet people, this began the Great Patriotic War, the bloodiest in the history of our country. Tens of millions of people died. Economy and culture suffered immense damage.

We are proud of the courage and steadfastness of the Red Army heroes and workers at home who not only defended the independence and dignity of their motherland, but also saved Europe and the whole world from enslavement.

Notwithstanding recent attempts to rewrite the chapters of the past, the truth is that the Soviet soldier set foot on German soil not to exact revenge on the Germans, but to fulfill his noble and great mission of liberation. The memory of the heroes in the fight against Nazism is sacred to us.

We gratefully remember the allies of the anti-Hitler coalition, the fighters of the Résistance and the German anti-fascists, who brought victory closer together.

Despite the terrible experiences of the World War, the peoples of Europe have managed to overcome alienation and find a way back to mutual trust and respect. They set course for integration in order to draw a line under the European tragedies of the first half of the last century. In particular, I would like to point out that the historical reconciliation between our people and the Germans in East and West of the now united Germany played a colossal role in shaping such a Europe.

It should also be remembered that it was German entrepreneurs who became pioneers of cooperation with our country in the post-war years. In 1970, a "deal of the century" was concluded between the USSR and the Federal Republic of Germany with the agreement on long-term gas supplies to Europe. This laid the foundation for constructive interdependence and subsequently made many great projects, such as Nord Stream, possible.

We hoped that the end of the Cold War would mean victory for all of Europe. Not much longer, it seemed, before Charles de Gaulle's dream of a united continent would become reality, and not so much geographically from the Atlantic to the Urals as culturally and civilizingly from Lisbon to Vladivostok.

Precisely in this sense - in the logic of creating a large Europe held together by common values and interests - Russia wanted to develop its relations with the Europeans. Both we and the European Union have been able to achieve a great deal in this way.

However, a different approach prevailed. Underlying this was the expansion of the North Atlantic Alliance, itself a relic of the Cold War. After all, it was created for confrontation at the time.

The root cause of growing mutual distrust in Europe lay in the eastward advance of the military alliance, which incidentally began with the de facto persuasion of the Soviet leadership to agree to a united Germany joining NATO. The verbal promises of the time, along the lines of "This is not directed against you" or "The block boundaries will not approach you" were all too quickly forgotten. The precedent was set.

Since 1999 there have been five more "waves" of NATO expansion. Fourteen other countries joined the alliance, including former Soviet republics, effectively ending any hopes of a continent without dividing lines.

Incidentally, one of the top SPD politicians, Egon Bahr, had warned of this. In the mid-1980s, he proposed a radical reorganization of the entire European security structure after German unity. With the participation of both the USSR and the USA. But neither in the USSR, nor in the USA, nor in Europe would anyone listen to him.

"We are open to fair and creative cooperation"

What is more, many countries have been presented with an artificial choice - to join forces either with the collective West or with Russia. In fact, this was an ultimatum. The consequences of this aggressive policy are vividly illustrated by the example of the 2014 Ukrainian tragedy.

Europe actively supported the armed unconstitutional coup in Ukraine . It all started with that. Why was that necessary? President Viktor Yanukovych, who was in office at the time, had already accepted all of the opposition's demands. Why did the USA organize this coup and why did the EU states support it without willing it and thus provoke the split within Ukraine and Crimea's exit from the Ukrainian state?

The entire European security system is currently in a desolate state. Tensions are mounting, the risk of a new arms race is palpable. We are missing out on enormous opportunities that the cooperation offers us. This is all the more important today as we all face the common challenges of the pandemic and its extremely serious social and economic consequences.

Why is this happening? And above all: What conclusions do we have to draw together? What lessons from history should we remember? In my opinion, the most important thing is that the entire post-war history of Greater Europe has proven the following: the prosperity and security of our common continent are only possible through the combined efforts of all countries, including

Russia. Because Russia is one of the largest European countries. And we feel our inseparable cultural and historical ties to Europe.

We are open to fair and creative cooperation. This also underlines our suggestion to create a common cooperation and security area from the Atlantic to the Pacific, which could include various integration formats, including the European Union and the Eurasian Economic Union.

I would like to emphasize once again: Russia advocates the restoration of a comprehensive partnership with Europe. There are many issues of common interest: security and strategic stability, health and education, digitization, energy, culture, science and technology, solutions to climate and environmental problems.

The world is dynamically evolving and is constantly being confronted with new challenges and threats. And we just can't afford to carry around the burden of past misunderstandings, hurts, conflicts and mistakes.

A burden that prevents us from solving current problems. We are convinced that we have to admit and correct all these mistakes. Our common and undisputed goal is to ensure the security of the continent without dividing lines and a unified space for equal cooperation and collective development in the interests of the prosperity of Europe and the whole world.

37

Negotiations with Russia

Nothing in Ukraine suggests that the Russian war will end any time soon. Yet, unlike the rest of the world, Ukrainian and Russian negotiators seem to believe in a possible diplomatic solution. "Everyone is waiting for news," Ukrainian President Volodimir Zelensky said in a speech on Monday after the latest round of talks between the two countries. The news is still some time away.

Monday's talks were not said to have failed; there was only a "technical pause," Zelenski's envoy Mikhailo Podoljak said. The fourth round of negotiations begins Tuesday. Earlier this weekend, Podoljak tweeted that progress had been made, now that the "Russians are no longer setting ultimatums, but are seriously listening to our proposals. He wrote that negotiations would henceforth be about "peace, a ceasefire, the immediate withdrawal of troops and security guarantees.

Putin has an interest in negotiating with Ukraine because if this invasion has made anything clear it is that Russia's military power is faltering. The invasion has been anything but smooth for Russia and has already cost the lives of thousands of soldiers.

The Russian advance has become a logistical disaster; Putin can turn the tide if he changes his strategy very quickly or "luck" must come to his rescue quickly. The Ukrainian army is offering fierce resistance, clearly has more knowledge of the terrain, and is getting better and more effective weapons supplied by the West. Moreover, Russia's economy is in free fall since the West imposed harsh sanctions.

Acceptable retreat

There are no signs yet that Russia is willing to abandon its invasion or withdraw troops, but it does appear that Putin wants to at least keep open the possibility of an "acceptable" retreat, should his war become too costly for him.

President Zelensky also benefits from negotiations, even if his opposition to the Russian invasion force is successful. The martial odds may be turning for Ukraine, and it is certainly not out of the question that Russia, after a disastrous start, may recover militarily and decide the war in its favor and, for example, take Kiev or raze it to the ground. The Russian invasion force, despite its many losses, is creeping closer and closer to the capital.

The humanitarian price Ukraine is paying in this war is already extremely high, as Russia tries to raze entire cities to the ground. The Russians are resorting to heavier and heavier means as the war continues. In the southern port city of Marioepol alone, it is estimated that more than 2,500 civilians have died. On Monday, several evacuation attempts failed in the city; some 160 civilians still managed to flee the area by car. The

Ukrainian city of Kharkov is constantly under Russian fire, the mayor of the city said on Monday. And the battle for Kiev has yet to begin. Moreover, Zelensky's pleas for a no-fly zone are not being heard in the West.

Global food supply at risk
Moreover, Ukraine's economy is suffering even more from the Russian invasion than Russia's economy is from Western sanctions. According to the IMF, the Ukrainian economy is at risk of shrinking by 35 percent and the global food supply (including Ukraine's) is at risk if the war does not end soon.

It is possible that Putin is hoping that Zelensky will give up Crimea and the self-proclaimed republics in eastern Ukraine in the negotiations, allowing him to sell the war to the Russians as a victory - Zelensky indirectly referred to this possibility last week.

But a real breakthrough seems unlikely until Zelensky and Putin speak directly to each other, something Zelensky has been urging for some time. On Monday, the Kremlin let it be known that the Ukrainian request to do so has not yet been received. If it comes to a meeting, it will probably take place either in Israel or in Turkey.

Sanctions!

"The United States has declared war on Russia economically and they are waging this war," Kremlin spokesman Dmitry Peskov said Wednesday. Moscow says it is seriously considering what to do after U.S. President Joe Biden decided Tuesday to ban imports of fossil fuels such as oil and gas from Russia. Earlier, the country imposed sanctions on Russian banks, executives and the country's central bank.

According to Peskov, Russia is and will remain a reliable energy supplier and will continue to supply energy flows. "But you see the bacchanals, the hostile bacchanals, that the West has sown. And that, of course, makes the situation very difficult and forces us to think seriously," the spokesman said.

The United States and the EU previously came out with tough economic sanctions because of Russia's invasion of Ukraine. Peskov announced Saturday that Western countries that have imposed such measures on Russia are guilty of "economic banditry," according to the Russian government.

Our own economy will get hit too!

But the war also has serious consequences for our own economy. Some economists are even warning that we could end up in recession in the United States and Europe. 'I'm afraid that's possible,' say the major economists. 'We already had uncomfortably high inflation eroding purchasing power, and it's getting much worse with rising oil and gas prices. Exports to Russia are also coming to a virtual standstill. And then we just have to hope that Putin doesn't completely turn off the gas tap in Europe.'

Can Russia handle this war?

Russia is the largest country in the world in terms of territory, but in terms of economy it is a small one, relatively speaking. Last year, the Russian economy amounted to about 1033 billion euros. That's actually only slightly larger than, say, the Netherlands, a country in Europe (850 billion euros), but smaller than, say, Spain (1200 billion) and more than three times smaller than Germany (3500 billion).

"Russia's economy runs on the export of raw materials, not only oil and gas, but also metals, grain and more," In 2021, oil and gas accounted for more than half (55%) of exports, and almost half (45%) of state revenues. "Energy is an important part of those exports; Russia is one of the largest gas and oil producers in the world."

It is unlikely that Russia's gas and oil exports to the West will come to a halt. "Also in the past, for example during the annexation of Crimea, physical energy supplies were never touched. One always stays far away from that."

But should it come to that, both Europe and Russia would be affected. "Because we in Europe need that gas and Russia depends on our payments."

The commodity economy of oil and gas production in particular has brought Russia a lot in recent years, bolstered by higher prices. As a result, the country has huge financial buffers. Currency and gold reserves have been boosted to $630 billion and the sovereign wealth fund holds $174 billion.

A ban from Swift

A harsh sanction hanging over Russia's head is the disconnection of international payments by disconnecting Russian banks from Swift. Banks worldwide use Swift for international financial transactions, and disconnecting a country makes payments and transfers virtually impossible. Without Swift, even withdrawing money from a Russian bank account could become problematic for ordinary Russians inside and outside Russia.

The EU is for the time being refraining from imposing the Swift sanction, it was announced this evening in Brussels. Some EU countries, such as Italy and Austria, fear the repercussions on their own economies because of major interests and investments of banks in Russia. Those fears were illustrated today by plummeting share prices of many major European banks. And it is also too early for the heavy sanction weapon Swift, on day 1 of the invasion, EU member states reasoned.

The UK, through Prime Minister Boris Johnson this evening, announced more sanctions on its own, including freezing assets of the largest Russian banks in the UK and exclusion from the UK financial system. Closure of Swift is still open as a sanction, Johnson says.

The United States is a strong supporter of the Swift sanction, not least because its own financial and economic interests in Russia are small, but is also waiting to do so. However, the punitive measures have been extended to more Russian banks and individuals.

At the request of the European Central Bank (ECB), European banks have indicated the size of their stakes in Russia, and therefore what is at stake and potentially lost. ING estimates that risk at about 4.9 billion euros, Rabobank thinks a few tens of millions. Only ABN Amro says there is nothing to lose.

According to the latest figures from BIS, the Bank for International Settlements, Dutch banks have $1.5 billion outstanding with Russian residents. For German and French banks, the claims are considerably more, $7.4 billion and $8.7 billion respectively. British banks have the highest risk at $13.6 billion, while U.S. banks have the least, only $366 million. From this point of view, Russia's financial restraint is costing the U.S. very little.

Russia and China economic relationship

Bypassing the financial lockdown is difficult, but not impossible. Banks are supervised by central banks and via Swift all movements can be followed, and especially the United States is keen on a hard financial lockdown. By secretly doing business with Russia anyway, banks risk fines and sanctions from the US.

Russia and China have been working on their own alternative Swift system since 2015, the Russians as a precaution since the Crimean invasion and the Chinese with a view to financial sanctions for skirmishes around Taiwan. Russia's SPFS system now handles 20 percent of domestic payments. The network is now limited to countries such as Belarus, Kazakhstan, Turkey and Iran, plus several dozen banks, including banks in Germany and Switzerland. All in all, it is still completely inadequate to replace Swift.

Russia and China are looking at whether the two systems can be connected, so that in the event of international sanctions the two can continue to trade with each other, out of sight of the US. Sanctions against Russia in the event of an invasion of the Ukraine could even speed up cooperation between the Russians and Chinese.

EU excludes 7 Russian banks from Swift payment system.

The Council imposed further restrictive measures in response to the Russian Federation's unprovoked and unjustified military aggression against Ukraine.

In particular, the Council prohibited the following:

the provision of specialized financial messaging services used for the exchange of financial data (Swift), to Bank Otkritie, Novikombank, Promsvyazbank, Rossiya Bank, Sovcombank, VNESHECONOMBANK (VEB), and the VTB BANK.

This prohibition will enter into force on the tenth day after its publication in the Official Journal of the EU and will also apply to legal persons, entities or bodies established in Russia whose ownership rights are more than 50% directly or indirectly held by the above-mentioned banks investing in, participating in or otherwise contributing to projects co-financed by the Russian Direct Investment Fund to sell, supply, transfer or export euro banknotes to or into Russia or to any natural or legal person, entity or body in Russia, including the Government and the Central Bank of Russia, or for use in Russia.

These decisions complement the package of measures announced by the High Representative on February 27 following the video conference of EU foreign ministers. Other measures include the supply of equipment and material to the Ukrainian Armed Forces through the European Peace Facility, a ban on access to EU airspace and airports for all types of Russian airlines, a ban on transactions with the Russian Central Bank, and a ban on broadcasting in the EU for the Russian state media Russia Today and Sputnik.

The European Union condemns in the strongest terms the unprovoked and unjustified military aggression of the Russian Federation against Ukraine, and demands that Russia immediately cease its military actions, withdraw all armed forces and military equipment from the entire territory of Ukraine and fully respect the territorial integrity, sovereignty and independence of Ukraine within its internationally recognized borders.

Do the sanctions hurt Putin?

The EU has frozen the assets they have stashed in Europe. "It's logical that you don't just look at the entourage, but you also look at the architects of the bloodshed,"

Not only is the European Union imposing sanctions on Russia and Putin, but so is the U.S. government. Among other things, President Biden announced that large Russian banks would no longer have access to their assets in the United States.

Biden believes that people who personally benefit from Russian policies should also feel the pain of such sanctions. Partly for this reason, the U.S. has put high-

ranking Russians and their family members on a
sanctions list.

But to also hit the Russian president himself in the
wallet, that's a lot trickier. Exactly how wealthy Vladimir
Putin is is completely unclear. Despite, or perhaps
thanks to, the fact that he has been in power for twenty
years, it is virtually impossible to get a handle on what
possessions and filled bank accounts belong to him.

No bank account abroad

According to data released annually by the Kremlin,
Putin earned about $140,000 (124,000 euros) as
president of Russia in 2020. The only possessions he
lists are three cars, a trailer, a 75 square meter
apartment and a garage. Putin also makes use of
another apartment in Moscow, of about 150 m2, and
two parking spaces.

Furthermore, Russian statesmen are prohibited from
having bank accounts abroad, a Kremlin spokesman
previously told Reuters news agency. How likely is it
that this is Putin's only asset and that, partly because of
this, it will be very difficult to impose financial sanctions
on him personally?

It is possible, writes business magazine Forbes, that the
lack of evidence of a wealthy Putin actually means that
he does not have much money and would only like the
whole world to believe otherwise. Nor does he need

that money at all, wrote a columnist at Bloomberg news
agency back in 2013; after all, he has an entire country
under his thumb that is at his beck and call.

There are two more theories about Putin's alleged
wealth that Forbes finds more likely. For the first, we
have to go back to 2003 and the arrest of oil tycoon
Mikhail Khodorovsky. Until his conviction for, among
other things, tax evasion and fraud, he was Russia's
richest man and an open critic of Putin.Chodorovsky
owed his wealth to his oil company Yukos, which was
cut up after his conviction. Speaking to Forbes,
American financier and Russia critic Bill Browder says
that after Khodorovsky's arrest, Putin struck a deal with
other wealthy oil coons.

Putin governs Russia like the Mafia

"Give me half your wealth, and you can keep the other
half," according to Browder, was the president's tactic.
"Otherwise Putin took 100 percent and threw you in
jail." Based on that deal, Putin would have been good
for $200 billion at the time, making him the richest man
in the world.

Another scenario from Forbes is the "mafia model.
Putin would award family, friends and other people
close to him big contracts and put them at the head of
big companies. In return, he would receive cash, shares
and other benefits. According to Swedish economist

Ander Aslund, Putin's assets would be worth between $100 billion and $130 billion based on this scenario.

How will the war develop?

In the early morning of Thursday, February 24, Russia officially entered Ukraine after much speculation and verbal threats. Associate Professor and Researcher in the History of International Relations Laurien Crump external link has been (been) a guest on several programs to interpret this historic event.

So as we have explained in the earlier chapters, the roots of this conflict lie in the 11 months after the fall of the Berlin Wall in 1989. "Gorbachev, the then leader of the Soviet Union, had grand plans for a common European home and a return of Russia to Europe," Among other things, he hoped that the Conference on Security and Cooperation in Europe (CSCE), now the Organization for Security and Cooperation in Europe (OSCE), would contribute to this. But, because the Gulf War was also being fought in those years, the focus increasingly came to be on NATO and the then European Community, and on how to expand them eastward. Thus it became clear early on that there was no place for Russia in Europe.

The Russian Perspective

"We must also understand that it is extremely threatening for Russia to have such a large military alliance armed to the teeth so close to the Russian border [should NATO expand, ed.]." The rhetoric in the West prior to the invasion did not help either: that the

West kept shouting loudly that Russia was going to invade Ukraine is, according to Crump, "an additional flame in the pan." And it is not only Russia that spreads propaganda. For weeks, people in the West had been talking about a Russian video that staged an attack by Ukraine. "Meanwhile, there is no evidence whatsoever that that video exists. You also see on the Western side a kind of war rhetoric, which leads to a vicious circle."

Speech of Putin in February 2022

On Monday, February 21, Putin delivered the speech announcing the raid. "I actually found it terrifying," says Crump. "Until recently, I thought there could still be a diplomatic exit route; now that seems passé. Putin makes the impression of being detached from reality." Until now, she could still place the Russian demands from a historical context, she says, but in his five-quarter-hour speech, Putin harks back to the Russian Empire, or rather the Kiev Empire, to which Ukraine belonged, thus denying Ukraine's right to exist as a sovereign state.

Crump also highlights the timing of the speech. On February 20, the Olympic Games ended, representing a period of peace. "Until then, there was opportunity for diplomatic negotiations and Putin could withdraw without losing face." The period of diplomacy now seems all but over.

Three scenarios

Crump outlined three scenarios for the advancement of the conflict, the first two of which have already come to pass. The first scenario was the recognition of Donetsk and Lugansk as independent regions, allowing Putin to send military forces into these areas. In the second scenario, Putin had his sights set on the entire Donbas region, an area in eastern Ukraine that is three times larger than Donetsk and Lugansk. The third scenario is that Putin wants to take all of Ukraine. "He has a lot of troops stationed in Belarus, a fleet in the Sea of Azov and he's already in Crimea, so Ukraine is already pretty surrounded. That seemed quite unlikely to me before, but after the speech it is now less far-fetched."

Reactions from the West

After Putin's speech and recognition of the two "republics," he announced a Russian "peace mission" in those areas. British Prime Minister Johnson now speaks of an invasion, while the European Union is still holding off on this. There is also disagreement about possible sanctions. "You see now within the EU that the former Soviet republics actually want to escalate immediately while other member states, want to phase in," Crump further explains.

Regardless of which sanctions the West will now impose, Russia has taken all possibilities into account in advance. For example, the Russian foreign minister said earlier that Russia is now used to their isolation and the

EU sanctions. It is therefore very important not to abandon diplomacy altogether, says Crump. "What I find dangerous now is that declaring the Minsk Accords passed, which Putin did today, is actually an implicit declaration of war." That means a diplomatic solution becomes enormously difficult. "If the diplomatic channels close and Russia is completely isolated, there will be further escalation and we will go to the third scenario anyway I fear."

Sanctions

On the night of February 23-24, around 4 a.m. the first reports of the Russian incursion into Ukraine come out. The European Union, the United States, and other countries announced tougher sanctions. British Prime Minister Boris Johnson, among others, is in favor of completely cutting Russia off from the international Swift system. This would exclude the country from international finance. Crump, too, thinks that would be an appropriate sanction, she says. "There is a lot of hesitation about it now, because it affects us too. But I do think: if this is not the right time, when is it? Now is the time to put a stop to it."

"It is the ultimate sanction, and it seems to me that it should not be waited for too long." Although she doesn't see it as a solution. "The word 'solution' is no longer appropriate; I don't see how this can be solved," says Crump. "More measures are possible, but they too will be counterproductive." As an example, she cites isolating Russia in international diplomacy.

Crump returns to the Swift sanction, which has been blocked by some European countries. The sanctions package that is now in place is firm, she says, "but in relation to what is happening now in Ukraine and to a Russian government and president who are actually out to overthrow the entire post-Cold War world order, I don't think it is nearly firm enough."

Buffer against NATO

Crump also points out that many Russians don't like the war either. "You can see that Putin has overplayed his hand tremendously on the domestic political level. A lot of Russians don't support [the war], and also Putinese Russians are now calling for it to stop." In her view, the threat from NATO remains the biggest problem. "I think Putin is really concerned about Ukraine. I don't think he wants to annex the Baltic countries or Poland or other NATO member states, but he wants to have a buffer there."

Putin is all about President Zelensky, she thinks, and in particular the democratization he stands for. "I think Putin's hope is to install a kind of puppet government, which at some point, with the help of Russians, but not with 190,000 Russian troops, can stay afloat, as has happened in many other countries in the area."

One hundred thousand Ukrainian refugees

NATO met for the first time on February 25, and decided to send troops to Eastern Europe. "NATO can hardly send troops to Ukraine itself," Crump says on News and Co (February 25), "then you're soon in a Third World War, that has to be prevented, of course, so troops are being sent to make sure that the Russians don't advance further westward and that NATO's borders, which run near the Baltic countries, that those are reinforced."

Meanwhile, thousands of Ukrainians have fled the country. Currently, estimates are that about a hundred thousand are refugees, but that could rise to four or five million. Crump suspects that most are heading toward Poland and other neighboring countries, where, unlike other refugees, they seem welcome. "The region" we normally associate with Syria or Afghanistan, something very far away, but "the region" is now Europe. And there's a large Polish community in Ukraine, so that's really seen as a brotherly people, so the Poles have a very different view of that."

Negotiations between Ukraine and Russia

On February 28, the first negotiations will take place between Ukraine and Russia. The chances of the two countries reaching an agreement are extremely low according to Crump. "First of all, they are taking place on the border with Belarus, which Zelensky did not want in the first place, because Belarus actually supports the invasion," she explains. Secondly, Putin has already said last night that he will put nuclear weapons in a state of readiness, so then you do negotiate with a very big knife on the table."

This is also seen as a crucial day for the cities of Kyiv and Kharkiv. "There is a steady advance by the Russians, on the other hand the resistance is much bigger than the Russians had estimated, tactical mistakes are being made on the Russian side, the airport near Kyiv is not yet in Russian hands and that is crucial. So it's not a done deal yet," Crump said.

Russian nuclear weapons in position

A day earlier, Putin threatened to use nuclear weapons. "The advance in Ukraine is not going as fast as he had hoped. I think he had hoped to have taken Kyiv a long time ago, so you're seeing a bit of a cornered cat making strange leaps here," says Crump. "And it's connected to a Russian doctrine, the Gerasimov doctrine, which sees nuclear weapons as a logical step in further escalation of a military conflict."

Whether Putin will actually deploy the nuclear weapons Crump does not dare say. "I don't think we can rule anything out at this point. The West is trying to be very careful about that, supporting Ukraine in all sorts of ways, with weapons, humanitarian aid, sanctions and so on, but not sending military troops there. So if it's up to the West, it doesn't mean that. On the other hand, on the Russian side, you see an appearance of an unpredictable president, who puts his own spin on everything. So what spin he's going to put on it, that's totally uncertain as of yet."

Unified international community

Crump answers the question of how the West should respond to these threats. "What you see is that the West is much less divided than Putin had hoped," she replies. "Even the European Union is extraordinarily united. Even a former ally of Putin, Hungarian Prime Minister Orbán has backed EU sanctions." She also mentioned a South Korea, Japan and Singapore, which are also imposing sanctions. "Even China's stance is notable," Crump said. China did not condemn the invasion, but abstained at the United Nations Security Council when it voted to condemn the UN.

Not much later, China offered itself as a "neutral mediator. "China is very much in a split," Crump explains. "They don't want to speak out against the invasion, but on the other hand they are now alone in that and the Chinese are always very much in favor of sovereignty and non-intervention."

China also has ties to Ukraine; it is Ukraine's first trading partner. According to Crump, there is a real chance that the country will therefore take on that mediating role.

International Court of Justice and International Criminal Court

There are increasing voices calling for Putin to be convicted through the International Court of Justice as well. "Lithuania has also added to the mix by bringing in the International Criminal Court," says Crump. Putin could then be classified as a war criminal and join a notorious list of other dictators.

Yet even this is unlikely to change Putin's mind. "He doesn't recognize all those courts, but it does add to his status as a pariah. And it could contribute to the further erosion of his support, not only in Russia but perhaps also within his own entourage."

Crumbling support

That support is already evaporating anyway, Crump says. "You can see on a number of fronts that support is evaporating very quickly." She cites Russians who may have previously voted for Putin but are now turning against him. But also more and more oligarchs, who previously sailed right by Putin's regime, see the war as a lost cause. Especially now that it will cost a lot of money because of the sanctions.

"And there are rumors, but of course this is much harder to verify, that there are also people in Putin's own entourage who think he is now going much too far." She points to television footage of uncomfortable conversations with people in the security council, which she says do not quite give the answer Putin had prepared with them.

The effect of sanctions

On March 2, Crump tells us that the economic sanctions will not deter Putin in the short term. They do, however, ensure that pressure will be exerted on him from below. "As a country, Russia can stay afloat financially I think, but the Russian people are already feeling it in their pockets. They can't withdraw money or transfer money abroad or receive money from abroad. They're not allowed to take much money abroad anymore, so protests are growing on an unprecedented scale in Russia as well."

Putin is creating an enemy in the people, Crump argues. "Suppose Putin does take Ukraine - he is already bombing all those cities - then he will soon have a country in which he has to establish a puppet government to implement regime change.

But a puppet government like that will have a very hard time dealing with a people who have resisted so vigorously, and who will continue to do so. You can win militarily, but if you don't win the hearts and minds, you can't govern that country," Crump said.

Energy Supply

President Biden announced that America will immediately stop importing Russian gas and oil. Crump explains the implications of these new sanctions, for Russia and Europe. "As long as it stays with America, it's not such a hard blow to Russia. It will only be a really hard blow if the European Union will also support this." In response to this move by the Americans, Russia threatened to turn off the gas tap of Nord Stream 1, the pipeline through which gas flows from Russia to all of Europe.

"This threat is effective from the Russian point of view because it allows Putin to be divisive. That is a breaking point because it has huge repercussions for Europe and EU countries, but not for the United States."

America, however, is well aware of Putin's tactics: "You can see that Biden in his speech is already trying to rhetorically anticipate this threat by saying that he does not expect the EU to follow him," says Crump.

In Europe, there is currently still enough gas supply to last through the end of the winter, and plans are underway, as in other countries, to reduce dependence on Russia.

Ongoing diplomatic negotiations
Meanwhile, Ukraine and Russia remain in talks. This, according to Crump, indicates that both countries are still interested in a diplomatic way out. She also explains

that that way out does involve a "very complicated balancing act.

"The conflict seems to be in a stalemate on both fronts, both military and diplomacy," she says. "That's not a coincidence. Both sides are hoping to score some more victories militarily, and then use those to force concessions at the diplomatic level."

Still, there is hope. Crump points out that the demands of both Ukraine and Russia have shifted slightly. "What Russian President Putin said at the beginning about this great Russian empire he envisioned and his idea of rapid regime change in Ukraine, those things now seem a bit further away. On the other hand, Ukrainian President Zelensky has said that it is also negotiable to take the idea of possible NATO membership for his country off the table and possibly consider Ukraine a neutral country with security guarantees." Also, Putin no longer insists on replacing the Ukrainian regime, Crump says. Moreover, subgroups are working on definitions.

"That assumes that certain topics are already being negotiated in a somewhat more concrete way, that a text is also being worked on." Although the chances are that it will still be about a temporary ceasefire and humanitarian corridors.

The absence of a ceasefire, however, is a less hopeful sign. "If you're really negotiating seriously, at a minimum there is a ceasefire to give an opportunity for reflection for a while and we haven't seen that so far," Crump told VTR News. She also warns that it is possible that Russia is using the negotiations as a propaganda tool. One indication of this is the fact that the Russian foreign minister said in Antalya that he has no mandate to talk about humanitarian corridors.

Crump says: "That suggests, first, that Putin is still firmly in control on that front, and, second, that the negotiation is more of a propaganda stunt from the Russians. Who can say, 'We're on a peace mission and we're trying to make peace,' than that a peace agreement is really being seriously sought."

What if Putin loses the war? And what if he wins? these are 8 eight scenarios of what potentially could happen...

The War in Ukraine The battle in Ukraine is going more difficult than Moscow expected. Yet Putin may yet win the war. But what will happen next? For Putin, the future does not look bright in almost all scenarios.

For the United States, it is certain: Vladimir Putin's plan was to capture Kiev within days and oust Ukrainian President Zelensky.

It didn't work out that way. More than two weeks after the start of the invasion, Russian tanks are on the Dnieper River, but a Russian victory on the battlefield is by no means certain.

With Putin's "special military operation" bogged down in bloody chaos, analysts are concerned with one question: how will this end?

No one can predict the future. But it is possible to draw up scenarios, not as a forecast, but as a first aid to thinking about Putin's war. The actual outcome will probably contain elements of different scenarios.

At the same time, however, it is also clear: in most scenarios Putin will not achieve what he intended.

SCENARIO 1

Putin loses the battle, loses his throne

The military campaign is completely bogged down, with ever-increasing Russian losses.

To replenish decimated units, Putin is forced to use conscripts. However, the resistance of Ukrainians cannot be broken. In a war, morale weighs three times as much as material, reads one of the many clichés about armed conflict.

After only two weeks, Russian state TV begins to ask tough questions aloud. With the first Russian conscripts killed, opinion in Russia soon turns against the Kremlin - state propaganda loses out to the Russian mothers mourning in Red Square.

Putin is forced to retreat behind the Ukrainian-Russian border. In the least-disastrous scenario for him, he gets to keep one or more of the three Ukrainian territories he controlled even before the invasion - Donetsk, Luhansk, Crimea. A consolation prize to limit the loss of face.

A loss could also turn out more disastrous for him: Putin loses Russia. An anti-Putin coalition of frustrated oligarchs, fumed paladins and disappointed top military officers emerges to topple the regime. Against that scenario, Putin has decimated political opposition and critical media in recent years. In this scenario, too, the war has disrupted a country and cost thousands of lives.

SCENARIO 2

Putin wins the war, but loses the peace

Western military analysts get it right: Russia is too strong in the end. After a faltering start in the first two weeks of the offensive, Putin brings the Zelensky government to its knees, possibly with a prolonged siege of cities. To break the last will to fight, the Russian military may deploy another tactical nuclear weapon, killing thousands at once.

Russia takes power in Kiev. Ukrainian President Zelensky cannot justify more death and destruction in his country and takes refuge abroad. The Ukrainian armed forces lay down their arms. Putin installs a regime led by ex-president Viktor Yanukovych, who fled in 2014.

Russian state media crow victory: Putin's mission is complete, historic Russia is one again. Slowly, moreover, the sanctions coalition that the West had forged is crumbling. Businesses and citizens in fickle democracies are beginning to feel the pain of lower profits and higher bills. Bakers are predicting a bread price of 6 dollars.

In a scenario favorable to Putin, he will sing out the sanctions. A major economic crisis does not necessarily mean the downfall of an autocratic regime, historian Tom Pepinsky found out.

More realistically, Putin may discover that although he has won the war, he has a huge problem on his hands. Ukraine is slightly larger than France. It's an area you can't simply occupy. "Even the 190,000 military personnel now deployed are insufficient to control the country," says Tim Sweijs, defense expert at The Hague Centre for Strategic Studies. "Just look at Western interventions in Iraq and Afghanistan.

Ukrainians have no intention of resigning themselves to the inevitable, especially after all the sacrifices. A resistance propped up by the West with weapons and money is turning Putin's war into a protracted guerrilla war that haunts Putin and the rest of his government. Russia languishes under an international regime of sanctions and isolation.

SCENARIO 3

Putin consolidates conquests, partitioning Ukraine

The Zelensky government must eventually flee Kiev and settle in Lviv, the new capital. Russian troops stop at the Dnieper River and dig in.

"There may come a time when Putin says, let's declare victory and go home," Sweijs says. A new national border is being drawn: southern and eastern Ukraine, including Crimea, are being annexed to Russia. De facto, "Russian-speaking" Ukraine comes under the Russian flag.

Putin would achieve a number of goals in this case, but he runs the risk that the rump state of Ukraine will definitively join the West.

SCENARIO 4

Putin attacks yet another non-NATO country

After Putin manages to stabilize the situation on the battlefield, his eager eye turns to other buffer zones. "It seems very likely to me that he will move on to Moldova, for example," says former NATO ambassador Timo Koster, former director of defense policy. The Moldovan region of Transnistria is pro-Russian.

With Belarus, which he already has in his pocket, and a friendly government in Kiev, he and tiny Moldova would have control over the border area on NATO's entire eastern flank, from Finland to Turkey. Putin is also forging a military alliance with Russia-friendly Serbia. In Belgrade, after two weeks of war, demonstrations were still held in his favor.

Putin is taking the extra risk because NATO has made it clear that it has no intention of defending non-NATO countries by force of arms. The red line is the NATO border.

When the United States threatened Putin with sanctions at the end of 2021, but also said that no soldiers would fight in Ukraine, "Putin saw that as a green light," Koster thinks. This could also apply to other non-NATO countries.

SCENARIO 5

Putin Tests NATO Solidarity

It may even be that Putin thinks the West will not respond with military force to an attack on a NATO country either, Koster suggests. It would be a huge step for Putin, but, says Koster, we can no longer afford not to think about it.

After Ukraine, then, the Baltic states come into the picture. After all, one theory about Putin's motivation is that he is not only concerned about Ukraine but wants to repair the historical accident of the Soviet Union's demise.

However, should Putin decide to invade the Baltic countries, he will immediately get into a fight with militaries of Western NATO countries stationed there. As a result, Russian aggression in the Baltic region almost immediately ends in an armed conflict with NATO. Sweijs does not consider this scenario likely.

"NATO has made it very clear that it will react adamantly to an attack on a member of the alliance."

SCENARIO 6

NATO intervenes in Ukraine, war with Russia

Both the U.S. and NATO have sent a clear message in recent weeks: the West does not want to get involved in the war in Ukraine. The question, however, is how tenable that position will remain if Putin burns Ukraine's major cities to ashes.

It is, wrote the American former intelligence officer Chris Chivvis for think tank Carnegie, a great challenge for the Biden administration to keep a cool head even then.

The West is faced with a dilemma: would intervention lead to provocation from Putin? "The deterrence by the West has not worked; the question is whether we want to continue to be deterred by Putin," says Koster. That question comes up again and again: with tougher sanctions, with whether or not to supply fighter jets, with the establishment of the no-fly zone that Zelensky begs for so passionately.

Public opinion can play a role here, Sweijs believes. "In the Western interventions of the past thirty years, the emotion 'we have to do something' was often the primary motive, without the consequences having been well thought through. A no-fly zone would be a very dangerous operation."

"The scenario I'm most afraid of," Sweijs says, is an unintended escalation. A mistake, a misinterpretation of the other person's actions, can have major consequences." The worst possible consequence then is the deployment of nuclear weapons.

SCENARIO 7

Putin and Zelensky come to an understanding

Half the world is ready to mediate between Kiev and Moscow. After Turkey, China, and Israel, South Africa came forward. Even former chancellor Gerhard Schröder, reviled in his own SPD for not wanting to distance himself from his friend Putin, flew to Moscow for mediation.

Initially, there is little reason for optimism. Temporary safe evacuation routes to allow civilians to escape from besieged cities only get off the ground after a number of rounds of consultations and with varying degrees of success.

A first meeting between the foreign ministers, Koeleba and Lavrov in Antalya, Turkey, yielded hardly anything. Lavrov even denied that Russia had invaded Ukraine. But they do talk to each other.
Russia demands recognition of Donetsk, Luhansk and Crimea as Russian and wants Ukraine to become a neutral, disarmed country and thus not join the EU or NATO. The demands are effectively unobjectionable for Zelensky.

Yet after two weeks of struggle, his government is hinting that something of neutrality is conceivable. NATO, Zelensky tells ABC, has made it clear that we are not welcome. He is pushing for membership in the EU. His chief of staff lets slip that formal transfer of Crimea and the separatist territories to Moscow can be negotiated, but that neutrality and demilitarization are non-negotiable.
For negotiations to have a chance of succeeding, there must be a "hurting stalemate," Sweijs says. Putin must realize that further warfare is a greater risk than a deal. Kiev will have to realize that defeating Russia is impossible. That situation does not seem to have been reached yet.

SCENARIO 8

Cold War 2.0

In all scenarios in which Putin remains in power, the West must set itself up for a long period of

confrontation, a new variant of the Cold War. Far-
reaching economic disengagement is then in the offing,
especially if Putin answers Western sanctions with
nationalization of Western companies. NATO and the
EU will have to adjust to high military expenditures and
a solid permanent military presence in Eastern Europe.

And Putin? For him, there are virtually no sustainable
favorable scenarios. Sweijs: "In all scenarios, Putin has
become the new Saddam Hussein or Assad."

Putin is destroying Ukraine

Two weeks after the invasion of Ukraine began, hundreds of thousands of people are trapped in cities pounded to ruins by Russian artillery. But more and more Russians are finding that they too are prisoners - not of shellfire, but of a full-blown dictatorship. Our foreign affairs expert Matthijs le Loux takes stock of the war in Ukraine.

The procession of Ukrainians seeking safe haven abroad swelled to more than two million this week. That's the fastest growing refugee influx in Europe since World War II, according to the UN.

Most of the refugees traveled to Poland (1.2 million) and other Eastern European countries. Many of them have relatives or acquaintances there. Some 210,000 fled to other parts of Europe.

These are the lucky ones. A total of 44 million people live in Ukraine. UNHCR, the UN refugee agency, expects a second big wave of refugees in the near future. That will probably include more people who cannot fall back on contacts abroad.

And then there are the millions of residents of cities that are now (mostly) surrounded by Russian troops. They have no way out until a ceasefire makes their escape routes safe enough. In the meantime, they are heavily shelled, much civilian infrastructure no longer works, and their supplies are running out.

Take the people trapped in besieged Mariupol, an estimated 200,000 to 300,000. They have had no access to running water, electricity or heating since March 2, while temperatures are around freezing.

The southeastern port city is an important strategic target for the Russians and is being flogged by bombings. According to the city administration, at least hundreds of civilians have died as a result of the war effort. Careful counts are impossible because emergency services can't keep up and phones don't work.

Refugees under fire

Humanitarian corridors (routes over which a cease-fire is called) are supposed to provide relief, but Russian willingness to silence the guns for a while appears to be low. Several evacuation attempts were aborted due to attacks, sometimes after less than an hour.

Refugees also come under direct fire: on Sunday, March 6, four of them, including two children, were killed by mortar fire in Irpin, a suburb of Kyiv. A team from The New York Times captured the attack. Photojournalist Lynsey Addario wrote that two scenarios were possible: the Russians deliberately targeted the evacuation route or showed a total lack of concern for civilian casualties.

Russia insists that it is not targeting civilians and and even says that Ukrainian "Nazis" are targeting their own civilians. That constant denial exudes a deep cynicism, since there is countless evidence to the contrary, from bombings of residential areas with no military value to incidents like the one in Irpin.

A ceasefire to evacuate civilians from the cities of Kyiv, Kharkiv, Sumy, Mariupol and Chernihiv seemed to be more successful than previous attempts on Wednesday, until a maternity hospital in Mariupol was bombed in the afternoon.

What does the ordinary Russian think about it?

How the invasion of Ukraine and all that ensues are received by the Russian people has occupied minds since the beginning of the invasion. But that question is gaining traction as the human toll of the war rises and more parts of Ukraine turn into smoldering ruins.

After all, Russians and Ukrainians are at least Slavic brother peoples, even the same people in the Kremlin's eyes.

Cities like Kyiv and Odesa are also part of the Russian national narrative. A Ukrainian acquaintance succinctly summed up the ties: "Just about every Russian has a Ukrainian cousin."

Attempts to gauge Russian public opinion run into the problem of the country's transition from authoritarian state to full-blown dictatorship. Russian journalist Sergei Dobrynin described that slipping in a gripping way in The Atlantic: "The decay of our society was so slow that many Russians could choose not to notice it. That was Putin's method: stick the knife in gradually. Less drama, same result."

The Kremlin has silenced the few independent news media that still operated in Russia and all other media outlets are proclaiming the government line.

Protesters are rounded up en masse and risk police brutality and high prison sentences.

Need for stability

Exactly who believes the deluge of government propaganda and who questions it is hard to say. The same goes for support for the war in general. Russia experts do see clear differences between young and old and between those living in urbanized areas and those in rural areas.

Younger people and city dwellers tend to be more international-minded, less dependent on state television, and more active on the Internet. Opposition to the war is more pronounced among them.

But such contrasts do not tell the whole story. An older Russian in the countryside can also understand perfectly well that the official story is flawed, but can decide, for example, to fall back on an effective survival strategy from Soviet times: nodding yes and making sure you are not above the surface.

Another important consideration for many older Russians stems precisely from the chaotic time after the fall of the Soviet Union: they need stability above all else.

Vladimir Putin knew how to deliver that in the past. And whatever else it would bring if Putin's regime were to collapse, more stability is not a likely outcome.

And, of course, there are also significant numbers of Russians who simply approve of the invasion, for example, because they share Putin's ideas of a "Greater Russia.

Two captive populations

The pressure on Russia's population is increasing from all sides. The economic sanctions from the West are unprecedentedly heavy. The effects are already being felt by ordinary Russians, who can buy less for their rubles, can no longer get into the subway by checking in with their cell phones, and can no longer get a Big Mac.

This will only get worse, especially if the West takes the Russian energy sector to task. Russia has become an international pariah and Russians abroad face harassment and violence.

Meanwhile, horrific information about the true nature of the battle in Ukraine is seeping through, from encrypted chat apps or phone calls to Ukrainian relatives. Moreover, the number of Russian soldiers coming home in body bags is likely to become significantly larger than the Kremlin will ever admit or be able to effectively cover up.

More and more Russians who have the means to do so are also becoming refugees: they are traveling to countries that still allow Russian flights, such as Turkey and Georgia, or crossing land borders into Finland or the Baltics.

Many analysts believe that the protests in Russia will grow. The Kremlin can then really only go one way, that of even more brutal repression. No grenades and missiles are descending on the Russian people, but in a way they are just as trapped as the Ukrainian ones. Putin has hijacked the plane, and all the occupants are at the mercy of what is dictated to him by his distorted worldview.

Russians lose troops and equipment, but not yet the war

After two weeks of war in Ukraine, two defense experts take stock. Their conclusion: the Russians are demotivated, suffering heavy losses and surprised by the resistance of the Ukrainians, but will - albeit with a delay - achieve many of their goals.

On the front near the city of Kharkiv, Russian Major General Vitaly Gerasimov was killed in action last Tuesday. He was leading the fighting against the Ukrainian army around the city of millions. The general's death is striking for several reasons.

First of all, what is a general doing at the front? Is there no one else who can lead the troops? "

It seems like in the Russian army they are running out of middle managers, soon they will have to send the commander in chief to the battlefield himself to give the orders," Bellingcat's editor-in-chief Christo Grozev wrote honourably on Twitter.

A defense specialist in the EU of institute Clingendael named Colijn is a bit more cautious in his analysis. "Things are not going smoothly there," he says. "Otherwise, the Russians wouldn't send a general to put things in order.

But for Russian clout, Gerasimov's death doesn't matter much in the end; they do have a thousand generals there."

80

Russians call on unsecured Chinese phones: 'Very vulnerable'

Another striking detail: an officer of the secret service FSB informed his superior on the other side of the border about the general's death via an unsecured line. Just last year, the Russian military introduced secure ERA cryptophones with much fanfare, but it turns out that they do not work in Ukraine because the 3G masts have been blown up by their own troops. And so they have to make calls with unsecured phones and local Ukrainian SIM cards.

So these calls were overheard by the Ukrainians. Bellingcat laid hands on those calls and found that the FSB agent at the front was calling his colleague Dmitry Shevchenko in the Russian city of Tula. When the latter heard that the general had been killed, a long silence fell. Shevchenko then began to curse profusely.

We spoke with a lecturer in military strategy at the EU Defence Academy that holds a PhD on the modern deception techniques Russia used in the annexation of Crimea in 2014. He follows the war in Ukraine closely. The fact that the Russians cannot communicate through secure connections makes them "very vulnerable," according to the lecturer.

"I understand that Russian soldiers even call each other on very cheap Chinese cell phones, which are very easy to break into. Then you make it very easy for your opponent to find out what you are doing."

Logistical problems slow advance, but do not prevent it
On social media there are not only many videos of abandoned and burned-out Russian tanks, but also of trucks carrying fuel and other goods. There are also stories of Russian soldiers looking for food and therefore looting stores and houses. "Those logistical problems are more likely to slow down an advance than prevent it entirely," says the EU defense specialist.

There will be "definitely logistical challenges," but you have them in every war. Therefore, he says, you shouldn't infer too much from burned-out trucks and stalled tanks. "We form our opinions based on the images we get to see, but that is only part of the reality. It may well be that there are far fewer problems elsewhere."

Ukrainian army distributes pinpricks and retreats to cities

The Ukrainian government circulated propaganda footage of Russian prisoners of war, each of whom said they thought they were engaged in a military exercise. There are also rumors that units from Belarus are refusing to go into action against the Ukrainians. "Young soldiers who don't want to fight lead to delays, but can easily be replaced,". "Or they put in planes with pilots who have had a much longer training and may be more motivated. You see that in Syria and saw it at the time with the war in Chechnya."

We can point out that the "masculine" Russian command structure can lead to demotivated troops. "In the Russian army, the commander is all-powerful. He determines in detail what should happen, lower officers and soldiers only execute. If things don't go well in an operation and you can't change the situation, you quickly walk around with your soul under your arm."

Big unknown is the Ukrainian army, which does not face the enemy in a traditional way, but rather throws pinpricks left and right and then retreats back to the cities. "It is difficult for the Russian army to fight against that. "As an army, you'd rather not enter a city; it's very difficult to conquer. There could be a sniper in every building, you'd need a huge force."

When Russians took Crimea in 2014, they used saboteurs, advance units that disabled installations and took politicians hostage. As a result, the Ukrainian government soon had its back against the wall. "They can forget about a repeat of those operations in Kyiv," says Bouwmeester. "If such saboteurs make themselves known, they will have the population against them."

Parties want to strengthen positions for negotiations in Turkey

On Thursday, negotiators from Russia and Ukraine will meet again, this time in the Turkish resort of Antalya.

The Ukrainians have a strong position because they are hard to grasp on the battlefield, show that they are capable of resisting and have a united population behind them. The Russians, at the cost of much human suffering and large flows of refugees, have gained a lot of ground in southern Ukraine and are in the process of encircling Kyiv. So they too will certainly not arrive in Turkey empty-handed.

According to Colijn, despite their losses, the Russians are still able to occupy and control Kyiv and can defeat the Ukrainians militarily. "That they are losing troops and equipment is against the odds, but on the grand total it is not that much," he said. That setback might actually encourage the Russian military leadership to want to continue the war dirty, i.e. with a lot of violence and civilian casualties."

Why is Kyiv so important?

The Ukrainian capital Kyiv is the main target of the Russian invasion. Russian President Vladimir Putin made it clear that there are not only strategic but also historical reasons for attacking the city. Why is Kyiv so important to Russians like Putin?

1. Kyiv is seen as the 'birthplace' of Russia

In the speeches in which Putin declared the invasion of Ukraine, he emphatically called Ukraine a historical part of Russia. The Russian president thus based his justification of the invasion on the common history of the two countries.

Like many Russians, Putin sees Kyiv as the "birthplace" of Russia. Kyiv had been the capital and namesake of the medieval Kiev Empire since 882. That empire covered much of present-day Ukraine, Belarus and Russia. It is considered by Russians to be the forerunner of today's Russia. The name Russia is derived from the Rus, the people who founded the Kiev Empire.

As the center of the Kyiv Empire, Kyiv became one of the most important and largest cities in medieval Europe. This happened centuries before, for example, the current major Russian cities of Moscow and St. Petersburg were of any importance. After the destruction of the city by the Mongols in 1240, Kyiv would never again live up to its former glory.

The rule of Kyiv and the surrounding area changed constantly in the following centuries. At the end of the eighteenth century, the region was incorporated by the Empire of Russia under the rule of Empress Catherine the Great. Many Russians point to that point as the moment when Ukraine finally became part of Russia.

2. Putin sees independence of Ukraine as huge mistake

Ukraine was one of 14 republics that gained independence from Russia after the collapse of the Soviet Union in 1991. It retained Kyiv as its capital, which meant the city was no longer part of Russian territory. But that did not mean that the common history suddenly disappeared.

To this day, there are close ties between Ukrainians and Russians. They are often even direct relatives of each other. Many Ukrainians speak fluent Russian in addition to their own language. Yet most of them feel truly Ukrainian, and therefore not Russian.

However, in the eyes of Russians like Putin, Ukraine still belongs to Russia in its entirety. They call Ukraine's independence a mistake that must be repaired at all costs.

3. Kyiv represents "the heart of Ukraine.

Kyiv is, of course, also strategically important to Putin and Russia. It is an unwritten rule of war that an attacked country is not defeated until its capital is taken. Consider, for example, the Taliban's seizure of power in Afghanistan. That is dated August 15, 2021, the day the jihadists took over the capital Kabul.

In the vast majority of countries in the world, the capital is also the city where the national parliament sits. The Netherlands - with Amsterdam as the capital and The Hague as the city where the parliament meets - is one of the few exceptions.

In Ukraine, too, the parliament - the Verkhovna Rada (literally Supreme Council) - has its seat in the capital. The Pecherskyi district where the parliament building is located is therefore also called the heart of Ukraine. The national parliament is the ultimate symbol of a country's self-government.

This is another reason why Putin is keen on conquering Kyiv. The Russian president said earlier that he does not see Ukraine as an independent country. So the symbols of Ukrainian independence are a thorn in his side.

4. 'Target number one' resides in Kyiv

Speaking of symbols of Ukrainian independence, President Volodymyr Zelensky has been staying in Kyiv since the start of the Russian invasion. He already let it be known several times that he will not leave the city.

Zelensky regularly shares photos and videos of himself walking through the streets and past famous buildings.

As head of state, Zelensky, like the parliament, is a symbol of Ukrainian independence. In addition, since the Russian invasion, he has become the poster child for Ukrainian resistance. He has turned out to be the biggest obstacle for Putin. He wants to install a pro-Russian government in Ukraine.

Zelensky has said that the Russians have made him their "number one target. According to Ukraine, three assassination attempts on the president have already been foiled since the invasion began.

The Russian convoy headed for Kyiv had been at a virtual standstill for the past few days, but on Friday new satellite images showed that the convoy had now disintegrated. Parts of the convoy have scattered across the region.

According to experts, Russian troops are preparing to storm the capital. This could take place sometime in the coming days.

Swiss banks and Russian money

Wealthy Russians have deposited a total of around 170 billion euros in Swiss banks. This was announced by the Swiss Association of Banks in a rare display of transparency.

The Swiss Bankers' Association told Reuters on Thursday that Swiss banks have between 150 billion and 200 billion Swiss francs worth of Russian money in their accounts. Converted, this amounts to a sum between 145 billion euros and 193 billion euros.

Switzerland is usually very reluctant to provide data on the identity of customers in Swiss banks, as it is known to discreetly manage assets of billionaires from around the world.

However, because of the Russian invasion of Ukraine, Switzerland has deviated from its regular "neutral" stance in international conflicts. The country has joined European sanctions against Russia.

Social Democratic politician Mattea Meyer, a member of Switzerland's National Council, has called for assets of Russian oligarchs in Switzerland to be frozen. "Some of that money belongs to oligarchs who are loyal to the Kremlin," she said. According to Meyer, Switzerland must "turn off the money taps."

Russian money in Swiss banks

According to the Swiss Association of Banks, the small 200 billion euros of Russian assets in the country is relatively small compared to the total assets foreigners have stashed in Switzerland. It is "less than 5 percent of the total," the banking club indicated to Reuters.

Switzerland's largest bank measured by total assets is UBS. This bank has exposure to Russia through lending of the equivalent of 613 million euros, according to its annual report for 2021.

Former ING boss Ralph Hamers is currently the top executive at UBS. Hamers indicated at a conference on Wednesday that UBS is looking at reducing risks related to the situation in Russia with its clients, Reuters reported.

Credit Suisse, the country's second-largest bank, reported in its annual report that some 1.5 billion euros worth of loans linked to Russia were outstanding at the end of 2021.

Switzerland has been widely criticized in the past for its banking secrecy, which would allow wealthy individuals with dubious backgrounds to keep money out of sight of investigating authorities.

In 2018, under intense international pressure, Swiss banks did move to share some information with tax authorities in other countries.

Ukraine and NATO

Russia has announced that online consultations with Ukraine will continue. Since Monday, representatives of both countries have been holding video talks to find a solution to Russia's invasion of Ukraine.

Military, political and humanitarian issues are being discussed, according to a spokesman for the Russian Foreign Ministry. The negotiations have not yet led to a breakthrough, but the parties appear to be making progress despite difficult talks.

Kyiv is demanding a ceasefire and the withdrawal of Russian troops. Moscow wants Ukraine to become a neutral country and not a member of NATO. The Russian delegation also wants Kyiv to recognize that Crimea belongs to Russia and that the renegade regions of Donetsk and Luhansk are independent states.

Ukraine and Russia reportedly approached each other in peace negotiations on Wednesday. The delegations are negotiating a 15-point peace plan, the Financial Times reported. The British business newspaper relied on three sources said to be involved in the talks.

A first draft of the peace agreement would include a ceasefire and withdrawal of Russian troops. That would be on the condition that Kyiv declares it will not allow Western military bases or weapons on its territory and abandons its ambition to join NATO.

The Russians would like a militarily neutral status for Ukraine, similar to Austria and Sweden. Those two countries are members of the European Union but not NATO. President Volodymyr Zelensky said Tuesday that Ukraine must recognize that NATO membership is out of the question.

NATO membership is out of the question for Ukraine for the time being. President Zelenski said so yesterday. Can the West then only look on? Six questions and answers about what NATO can still do to help Ukraine. And what, above all, they should not do.

For a long time it was a great wish of Volodomir Zelensky, the president of Ukraine: to become a member of the military alliance of the West. Because if Ukraine were a member, the West would help militarily to defeat Russia. But that wish can be crossed. NATO does not want Ukraine to join, so the country must look for other allies militarily.

1. Why can't Ukraine join NATO?

Before we look at who those allies could be, first the question of why membership is out of the question for Ukraine. We discuss it with Laurien Crump, senior lecturer in International Relations at Utrecht University. "NATO doesn't want a war with Russia," says Crump. "That's also one reason Ukraine has never joined before."

"According to Article 5 - an attack on one member state is an attack on all - NATO would have to come to Ukraine's aid in a war. That risk, which is now a reality with the current war, is too great for member states."

"Zelensky has now understood that message. The day after the Russian invasion of Ukraine, he asked if his country could join, but there was a deafening silence on the NATO side," says Crump. "And he says now he doesn't want to beg for it on his bare knees."

There is another reason at play. "A hard requirement for NATO membership is that a country has to solve internal and external problems before it can become a member. That is, NATO does not want to import insecurity from another country. When Putin annexed Crimea in 2014, it had actually already happened. Because of that level of insecurity, Ukraine cannot become a member of NATO."

2. And that no-fly zone. Why isn't that coming, too?

"Such a no-fly zone may sound very friendly, but that means that if Russia flies in Ukrainian airspace, NATO has to shoot down the Russian aircraft. And that, in turn, means that NATO is still interfering in the conflict," says Crump.

"During the fight against Saddam Hussein, a no-fly zone was chosen in Iraq. But then it was a situation that only took place in Iraq. That is different in Ukraine. The danger there comes from a neighboring country. That means in this case that you have to enforce a no-fly zone not only in Ukraine, but also over Russia. If you want to help NATO into the abyss, you have to do that."

3. The Prime Minister of Poland, after his visit to Kiev, talks about a NATO peacekeeping mission. What is that?

"I think he's just shouting something,". "We are blessed with politicians who do not know what exactly this is about. You can't have a wartime peacekeeping mission. It can only be done once a peace agreement is signed. Then a mission can ensure that the country in question remains stable."

"And even if there were a peace agreement, NATO cannot be the organization that oversees it

"Because NATO is exactly the problem. Then Russia says, Look, NATO is occupying Ukraine."

4. The prime ministers of the Czech Republic and Slovenia were also in Kiev. Can they help Ukraine?

"Supplying weapons is a two-sided affair. There is no such thing as NATO weapons.

The Americans, for example, also supply them. But sending troops? If you want to commit suicide, you can.

Should a Czech Republic, Poland or Slovenia do so, that country becomes part of the battle. And then what does NATO do if Poland is attacked?"

"You notice that the idea of a NATO peace mission is already causing tensions within that organization, and also within the European Union. The EU already said that the countries mentioned had not consulted with them. Then you know enough. They don't see the point, because then the Western alliance will still be involved."

5. What can NATO do to help Ukraine, though?

"Not much, because of the last thirty years of budget cuts. There are no longer large combat units with a lot of firepower.

What can still be done is to send radar planes. They use them to see what is happening in Ukraine. But mainly to see if there will be an attack against NATO."

A statement from Brussels is also a possibility. Today there is a NATO meeting there with the defense ministers of the member states. "Such a statement is meant to keep the morale of Ukrainians high," he said.

"And it is a signal to Russia. At the time of negotiations, any support is important. But in fact, NATO has to operate very cautiously now in particular."

6. What should NATO especially not do?

"Any step that causes further escalation, you should not
want. For example, today America is saying that Putin is
a war criminal. That is morally right, but very awkward."

"The same thing happened with Syrian President Assad.
The West said, 'He's a war criminal, so we won't talk to
him anymore.' That too is morally justifiable, but if
there is no more talking, then it is rational for the
person who is called a war criminal to continue
fighting."

"I fear that the West is going to do things that seem
right, but turn out wrong. Things that will make it
impossible to talk to Putin anymore. That you want him
on trial eventually is clear. But first let the war be over."

Upcoming food shortages

The grain in Ukrainian fields is in good shape and the country will have enough bread this year. This is what Ukrainian Agriculture Minister Taras Dzoba said on Wednesday.

Ukraine is one of the main producers and exporters of grain worldwide. Because of Russia's invasion of the country, there are concerns about grain production.

Analysts in the country previously warned that grain production could drop sharply because of the invasion, as it would leave less farmland to sow in. However, the crops that are now in the fields are doing well. Ukraine has enough bread this year, despite the difficult conditions under which work must be carried out on the land, the minister said in a statement. However, prices are likely to be higher because of the war.

Connoisseurs predicted earlier this week that almost 40 percent less farmland could be sown for grain because of the war. Ukraine harvested a record 86 million tons of grain in 2021. Ukrainian President Volodimir Zelensky said last week that the country should sow as much grain as possible this spring.

Ban on grain exports in Ukraine

Ukraine previously imposed a ban on the export of several types of grain. Rye, barley, buckwheat and millet, among others, may no longer be exported, the government in Kiev decided. By doing so, the government hopes to keep enough food for its own people and its army in times of war. In recent weeks the prices of grain have already risen significantly.

The export of sugar, salt and meat has also been restricted by Kiev. The bans last until the end of the year.

Wheat prices rose sharply in early March, following the recent rally due to the war in Ukraine. The Russian invasion and sanctions against the country have brought wheat exports to a virtual standstill. This puts supplies to other countries in jeopardy.

Ukraine and Russia account for more than a quarter of the world's wheat exports.

This summer, record harvests in North America and other parts of Europe will be critical to slowing further price increases. As flows from the Black Sea region are squeezed by the war, many buyers are considering futures contracts for Australian wheat. These are already placing orders well into the third quarter, according to trader CBH Group.

Food processing companies are diligently looking for alternatives to sunflower oil. Its stocks are good for about four to six more weeks and then it will run out.

That's because of the war in Ukraine, which is a major producer of vegetable oil.

"We're going to notice that in two ways," states a spokesperson for the industry association. "First, the sunflower oil shelf in the supermarket will be empty." In addition, sunflower oil will also disappear from a variety of products. "Producers are already looking for alternatives. Sunflower oil is used to fry chips and fries, for example, but it is also found in margarine, cookies and in baby food. It's very versatile."

Alternatives could include rapeseed oil, linseed oil or palm oil, the spokesman explains. What works depends on the product and how the oil is used. In addition, the labels and packaging must also be adjusted if another product, rather than sunflower oil, is used. This has consequences for the ingredient list, but also possibly for the nutritional value.

Switching to other ingredients and adapting the packaging costs companies money and inevitably results in higher prices. "The demand for those alternatives is increasing and so they are also becoming more expensive.

The extent to which companies can absorb all the price increases themselves is limited," says the spokesperson. Incidentally, various packaging materials such as tin and cardboard are also becoming more expensive due to the war in Ukraine.

'We feed the country'
One of the country's largest warehouses full of
foodstuffs near Kiev has been bombed. It is unclear
whether the warehouse in Marioepol is still there and
whether the refrigeration is still working. Distributing
food products in the country is life-threatening for the
drivers. Tanks drive over the fields where sowing is
supposed to take place.

"But the business goes on," says Rich. MHP (Myronivsky
Hliboproduct) in Ukraine employs 30,000 people. The
company has large chicken farms all over the country
and nearly 400,000 hectares of land producing wheat,
corn, sunflowers and other crops.

The company says in normal times it accounts for 50
percent of Ukraine's food production. "But now it is 100
percent. We are the only ones still operational. We are
feeding the country."

Australian Rich currently works with a handful of
employees from Slovenia. Most of his management is
still in Ukraine, though.

Phone network broken

"It's difficult, but during the Covid pandemic we learned
to work remotely. I have a lot of phones, and
communicate through Whatsapp, Signal, Zoom and
Teams. This is the only way we are in touch with our

local people. The telephone network has largely disappeared. So everything goes through the Internet."

By the way, the company's website is down for fear of Russian hackers as a precaution. All it says is a statement of support for Ukraine's troops.

Starving
Rich is concerned about the growing difficulties of distributing the products across the country. Where a truck normally took two hours to drive, it now takes ten. That's because of inspections, damaged bridges and roads.

"It's hard to find drivers willing to go on the road. It has become a minefield everywhere and difficult to get trucks back and forth without losing lives."

According to Rich, it is a clear plan by the Russians to cause food shortages in Ukraine. "They are bombing distribution centers. Those centers are supposed to supply supermarkets. This is a policy of starvation."

The next few weeks are crucial for food security in Ukraine, Rich says. It's the time to sow seeds.

Russians take away food

"A lot of grain is made by small farmers. They don't have their fertilizer yet. Problem is, they also don't have the money for it or can't access it because assets are frozen. And without fertilizer, production is many times lower. As a large company we do have everything we need. But it has to calm down before we start sowing."

He does also fear that what food is in storage now could just be confiscated by the Russians where they can. "Their logistics don't work well. So anything they get their hands on, they will eat themselves."

"The Ukrainians are very patriotic. They want to fight. It's going to be terrible."

If there can't be enough sowing in the next few weeks, the whole world is going to notice, Rich argues.

"Fifty percent of the world's sunflower oil comes from this region. A quarter of the wheat and 20 percent of the rapeseed. Then when you consider that much of that serves to feed animals in the EU and Britain those percentages of how important it is are even higher. The impact on prices of food becomes unimaginable with the problems here."

'It's going to be terrible'

In the south and west, Rich says staff are still relatively safe. "In the Kiev area, it's very difficult. We have also evacuated a large part of our staff in the east of the country to Poland. With the Red Cross, we got buses there to pick them up." Most of them are women and

103

their children. Most of the men are not allowed out of the country.

Rich fears that the war will last a long time. And that a shortage of food will play a leading role in it. "The Ukrainians are very patriotic. They want to fight. It's going to be terrible."

Russia looks at 'parallel imports' after companies leave

Russia is looking at so-called parallel imports to get goods from Western companies. This means that those goods are not imported with the permission of Western companies, but are bought from other companies, which in turn have bought them with that permission. Normally, this type of import, also known as gray import, is not allowed.

The Russian competition authority says it had a conversation with the director of Russia's main online store Wildberries, where the legalization of parallel imports was discussed. Both parties agreed that both Russian consumers and businesses would benefit.

Because of the sanctions and anti-Russian sentiment, many Western companies no longer supply their products to Russia. As a result, Russian shopkeepers have fewer and fewer goods to sell. Small and medium-sized companies in particular could be helped if they could buy batches of goods from countries that do want to trade with Russia.

According to Wildberries' top woman Tatyana Bakalchuk, gray imports are "particularly important for goods such as medicines, food and children's items. Although those goods are allowed to trade with Russia as usual, some Western companies are choosing not to do business with the country after the invasion of Ukraine. However, most pharmaceutical companies have indicated that they will continue to supply medicines as usual.

Baltic states and Bulgaria expel Russian diplomats

The Baltic states and Bulgaria are expelling a total of 20 Russian diplomats because of the war in Ukraine. Bulgaria has designated ten diplomats as persona non grata, while Lithuania expels four diplomats and Estonia and Latvia three each.

The Russian diplomats in Bulgaria have been given 72 hours to leave the country for activities that violate their diplomatic status. Latvia reports exactly the same reason, saying it also takes into account Russian aggression in Ukraine.

Estonia says of the diplomats that they "directly and actively undermined Estonia's security and spread propaganda justifying Russia's military action. Lithuania lets it be known that it wants to be in solidarity with Ukraine. The Baltic countries have coordinated their action.

Earlier this week Slovakia already decided to expel three Russian diplomats. At that time Russia said it would respond to the 'unjustified' step. There will also be a response to the 'hostile' expulsion of the diplomats from Bulgaria, the Russian embassy in Sofia has said.

Russian central bank keeps interest rate at 20 percent

Russia's central bank maintains key interest rate at 20 percent. Since the country invaded Ukraine, it has been under heavy economic sanctions. To counteract the fall in the Russian ruble and higher inflation, the interest rate was more than doubled at the end of last month.

Russian President Vladimir Putin said earlier this week that his country had survived an "economic blitzkrieg" of international sanctions. In doing so, he did warn that Russia will face rising unemployment and inflation as it adjusts to the new reality. The new situation will require 'profound structural changes' in the Russian economy, according to Putin.

Putin acknowledged that "rising prices are seriously affecting people's income. He said the government has sufficient resources to cover the costs without printing money. In doing so, he did not go into detail.

Russian central bank boss Elvira Nabiullina is due to comment on the interest rate decision on Friday afternoon. Putin wants to reappoint the economist, who has led the central bank since 2013.

German minister seeks alternative for Russian gas in Gulf region

Germany's Minister of Economy and Climate is traveling to the Persian Gulf this weekend as part of efforts to reduce Germany's dependence on gas from Russia. Qatar, Minister Robert Habeck's first destination, is one of the world's largest exporters of liquefied natural gas. This so-called lng could be an interesting alternative for German energy supplies, but currently Qatar's gas goes mainly to Asia.

Germany needs more liquefied gas for the lng terminals it wants to build, Habeck pointed out. However, he added that this fossil fuel should only be used "temporarily and in the short term," as a kind of intermediate stage towards more sustainable energy sources. The Bündnis 90/Die Grünen politician sees opportunities in a transition from conventional natural gas to green hydrogen and also said that the war in Ukraine has made this transition more urgent.

Port of Rotterdam: container traffic in particular affected by sanctions

In the Port of Rotterdam, container transport in particular is feeling the impact of the sanctions imposed on Russia because of the war in Ukraine. According to the Port Authority, the uncertainty about the sanctions is partly responsible for terminals and shipping companies no longer accepting or handling containers with destination Russia at all.

Approximately 8 percent of container transport through Rotterdam is linked to Russia. A large number of goods are subject to an export ban, including goods that can be used for both civil and military purposes, the so-called 'dual-use goods'. Because it is not always clear what is and what is not covered by the sanctions, many companies choose in advance not to process this cargo. Another factor is that it is not certain if and when customs, which is responsible for inspections, will release the containers in question.

Another point that makes companies cautious is that it is not clear how the war in Ukraine will develop. Payment risks also play a role in this. According to the Port Authority, it is unclear what the developments in Ukraine will mean for trade flows in the coming period.

The import of energy such as crude oil, oil products, liquefied natural gas (lng) and coal is not affected by sanctions at this time. Of the nearly 470 million tons of transshipment in Rotterdam, 62 million tons is Russia-oriented, according to the Port Authority. Currently, about 30 percent of crude oil comes from Russia and a quarter of lng. In addition, Russia accounts for 20 percent of the oil products and coal shipped in.

Russia also exports steel, copper, aluminum and nickel through Rotterdam, among other things. For the time being, this also does not fall under the trade restrictions announced by the European Union.

www.ingramcontent.com/pod-product-compliance
Lightning Source LLC
Chambersburg PA
CBHW070542160726
48003CB00004B/1836